MW01533522

How To Be A Options Trading King

Andrew Johnson

© **2017**

Sign Up & Join
<u>Andrew Johnson's</u>
<u>Mailing List!</u>

*EXCLUSIVE UPDATES

*FREE BOOKS

*NEW REALEASE
ANNOUCEMENTS
BEFORE ANYONE ELSE
GETS THEM

*DISCOUNTS

*GIVEAWAYS

FOR NOTIFACTIONS OF
MY *NEW RELEASES* :

Never miss my next FREE PROMO, my next NEW RELEASE or a GIVEAWAY!

© Copyright 2017 by Andrew Johnson - All rights reserved.

The following eBook is reproduced below with the goal of providing information that is as accurate and as reliable as possible. Regardless, purchasing this eBook can be seen as consent to the fact that both the publisher and the author of this book are in no way experts on the topics discussed within, and that any recommendations or suggestions made herein are for entertainment purposes only. Professionals should be consulted as needed before undertaking any of the action endorsed herein.

This declaration is deemed fair and valid by both the American Bar Association and the Committee of Publishers Association and is legally binding throughout the United States.

Furthermore, the transmission, duplication or reproduction of any of the following work, including precise

information, will be considered an

illegal act, irrespective whether it is done

electronically or in print. The legality

extends to creating a secondary or

tertiary copy of the work or a recorded

copy and is only allowed with express

written consent of the Publisher. All

additional rights are reserved.

The information in the following pages

is broadly considered to be a truthful

and accurate account of facts, and as

such any inattention, use or misuse of

the information in question by the reader will render any resulting actions solely under their purview. There are no scenarios in which the publisher or the original author of this work can be in any fashion deemed liable for any hardship or damages that may befall them after undertaking information described herein.

Additionally, the information found on the following pages is intended for informational purposes only and should thus be considered, universal. As befitting its nature, the information presented is without assurance regarding its continued validity or interim quality. Trademarks that mentioned are done without written consent and can in no way be considered an endorsement from the trademark holder.

THIS BUNDLE INCLUDES THE FOLLOWING BOOKS:

Options Trading: A Beginners Guide to Option Trading Unlocking the Secrets of Option Trading

AND

Options Trading:The Ultimate Guide to Options Trading Uncovering Options Trading Profit Making Secrets

TABLE OF CONTENTS

Options Trading: A Beginners Guide to Option Trading Unlocking the Secrets of Option Trading.................................**13**

Description...............................*13*

Introduction.................................*17*

Chapter 1: Understanding Trading as a Whole..............................*20*

Chapter 2:Options Trading in a Historical Sense.............................*27*

Chapter 3: The Basics of Options Trading 40

Chapter 4: How to Get Started with Options Trading..............................*56*

Chapter 5: The Different Types of Stock Options..................69

Chapter 6: Choosing Index Options..........82

Chapter 7: Choosing Currency Options.....96

Chapter 8: ETF and The Future Options. 109

Chapter 9: Options Trading Strategy Terms 123

Chapter 10: The Options Trading Strategy 136

Chapter 11: Ensuring Success with Options Trading..................149

Chapter 12: Is Passive Income Possible with Options Trading?......................165

Conclusion..................173

Options Trading:The Ultimate Guide to Options Trading Uncovering Options Trading Profit Making Secrets..........175

Description...175

Introduction..182

Chapter 1: The Mindset of the Successful Options Trader...186

Chapter 2: Tips for Success.......................212

Chapter 3: Mistakes to Avoid...................234

Chapter 4: Analyzing Your Trades..........250

Chapter 5: Option Trading Strategies to Consider..262

Chapter 6: Advanced Strategies to Try...285

Conclusion..315

OPTIONS TRADING: A BEGINNERS GUIDE TO OPTION TRADING UNLOCKING THE SECRETS OF OPTION TRADING

DESCRIPTION

Trading, in general, can be confusing. Options trading can be even more confusing. This is especially true if you don't know what you are doing or if you have never dealt with trading in the past.

Just because you're a beginner, though, doesn't mean that you have to stay that way. When you read this book, you will be able to learn all of the basics that you need to help make your options trading career more successful. I can't guarantee that you will make money from options trading, but I can guarantee that this book will provide you with the tools that you need to start making money.

As you are reading through the chapters, think of the different ways that each of them applies to your situation. If you have not started building capital up yet, consider how you will be able to do that. If you have not been able to find a broker, consider that.

This book is full of ideas on how you can make sure that you are going to be the best options trader possible. Your portfolio will be filled with options trades that are good and profitable. You will also learn the basics that you need to know about hedges and even futures trading.

Are you ready to take your beginner knowledge to the next level?

INTRODUCTION

Congratulations on downloading your personal copy of *A Beginner's Guide to Options Trading*. Thank you for doing so.

The following chapters will discuss some of the many different aspects of options trading.

You will discover how important it is to make sure that you are getting a good deal on the trades that you do.

The final chapter will explore how options trading can work to give you passive income.

There are plenty of books on this subject on the market, thanks again for choosing this one! Every effort was made to ensure it is full of as much useful information as possible. Please enjoy!

CHAPTER 1: UNDERSTANDING TRADING AS A WHOLE

Trading is essentially the process of making money through smart decisions. You can buy and sell different pieces of companies and businesses, known as shares, through the process of trading. The beauty of this is that you are able to make money from it.

When you are trading, you will first start out by making an investment. This can be a large one or a small one, but most people start with just a small one so that they are not going to be out a lot of money if they happen to make a poor choice with the investment (as beginners often do). The point of trading is to have as little risk as possible when you are trading so that you will be able to keep things as profitable as possible, or break even at the very least.

After someone has initially invested in something, they will then allow it to sit for a period of time. Some people choose to just trade through the course of one day. They don't make a lot of profit at once, but they normally have many different investments that they are working with at any time. When they do this several days a week – known as day trading – the profits typically build up. Others, though, want to let their investments sit for a week, a month, a year, or sometimes even longer. When they do this, they watch the price of the investment closely and then when it is at its highest, they sell their shares for profit.

If you are planning to start trading at any point in your life, you need to know that there are differences in trading types and that you should stick to one type of trading. For example, if you have chosen options trading as your niche, you should not try to start real estate trading or investing in anything else other than what you started with.

Picking a niche is the only way that you will be able to turn into a professional. You need a niche so that you can focus on one thing. When you focus on only one thing, the experience that you gain is a lot more focused, a lot more valuable, and a lot more profitable. As a result, by working with niches, you also become a better investor.

Picking a niche like options trading is a great way to get started with trading and is something that most people will be able to handle when they are just getting started in their trading career. It is important to note that options trading isn't necessarily easy. In fact, it's not easy at all, and can be quite risky. However, it is something that you can learn in a short period of time.

If you are going to start options trading, you need to learn as much as possible about it so that you will be able to be successful at it; otherwise, you run the risk of making a poor investment and losing big. That's where this book comes in.

CHAPTER 2: OPTIONS TRADING IN

A HISTORICAL SENSE

Options trading is something that is currently very popular, and it is one of the biggest forms of financial trading in the world. Billions of dollars in contracts are traded on a yearly basis, and that is something that, obviously, has a huge effect on the economy in all areas of the world. Because of this, many believe that options trading in its current form has been around for hundreds of years, but that simply isn't true.

Options trading, as we know it today, started just about 50 years ago and has ballooned since then, becoming bigger and offering more trading opportunities for people who are thus interested. Because of the risky nature and historical tendency to lead to speculative bubbles, some investors are still leery about options trading.However, modern options trading is relatively safe.As an example of how young modern options trading is, the Chicago Board Options Exchange is one of the oldest modern options exchanges and it has only been around since the 1970s.

Looking at Futures vs. Options

Futures and options are really close to being the same thing. The biggest difference lies in the way that you are able to carry out the contract. For example, you are able to sell your options at any time that you want. With futures, you have to wait until the end of the contract if you want to be able to sell the investment and start to profit off of it.

Futures are very limiting while options are very flexible in terms of selling for a profit.

Ability to Sell Your Options

One of the biggest benefits to using options is that, as I said, you can sell them at any time that you want within a certain timeframe delineated in the contract. However, this also means that you need to make sure that you are going to truly profit from the options contracts that you have established.

Because there are so many different aspects that go into trading, especially when you have somethingso functional and important as options contracts, you will be able to look at the different key points of shares and contracts, as well as the way that they are building up value while you have them. Once you've evaluated everything, if you want to sell your options and the price is at a good point, you can stand to make a huge profit off of them.

Change in the Way That Options Work

Throughout time, people recognized that there was a need to have a way to speculate on future values. Many investors liked the way that trading worked and they especially liked the way that futures worked, but they did not want to have to wait until the end of the contract to be able to profit from the trades. This was something that they always kept in mind, but it took off when options trading became a reality. There are many ways that options trading works to help enterprising investors out, and allowing them the chance to sell their investments off at anytime that they want at a certain price point gives them the flexibility that many people hope for when they are trading and when they are doing different things.

Options in the Past

Despite the fact that options are a fairly new concept in the world of modern trading, the idea behind options trading is ancient. As far back as ancient times, people were speculating on certain markets. This was something that the modern traders to base their options trading ideologies on, and it allowed them the chance to make sure that they were truly doing things the right way by comparing their set-up to the mistakes of the past, such as the Dutch Tulip bubble.

Options trading historically served the same purpose it does today: a way for people to make money off of their intuition for judging market directions. While they did not necessarily call it options trading at the time and they certainly did not have the technology that is available today, the principles behind it were the same.

Having Regulations for Options

When futures trading first started, there were a lot of regulations for it, and people had to follow each of these regulations to make sure that they were going to be able to get the best experience possible when it came to the trading opportunities. In other words, the regulations served both the investors and the economy by preventing speculative bubbles.

The same is true for options trading. However, with options trading,the regulations didn't really start to pop up until after the *concept* of options trading had been long developed. Because of this, the process for developing regulations was a little different than it had been for futures, as the process for developing regulations for options trading had been based in the historical mistakes of speculative trading.

Obviously, having the ability to look at past options trading scenarios was helpful when the regulations were being made. Looking to the past will invariably teach you a lot about the future. The same is true for options trading. There are a number of regulations in place based on the early mistakes of proto-modern options trading and early speculative markets.

In other words, the regulations for options trading may seem rather extensive, but they are as they are for very good reason.

CHAPTER 3: THE BASICS OF OPTIONS TRADING

There are a few things that you need to know before you start options trading. You need to know what options trading is, the basic language you will find in the trading world, why people choose to work with options contracts, the different orders that you can use with options trading, and the way that options work.

Definition of Options

Options are a type of trade that is in contract form. The buyer of the contract is then able to sell the asset that comes along with the contract at a specified time for a specified price. Essentially, it's a promise from one person to another to either buy or sell something at a given price, regardless of its real market price, at a certain point. The price does fluctuate both up and down when it comes to the total value of the options, as a response to the market price and the contract price. Because of this, you can be sure that you will almost always make a profit on the options if you know the right way to buy them and know the specific terms of the contract.

The biggest thing with options is that they do have an expiration date. If you do not have a chance to sell it off before that time, then you will lose your money because the contract is void.

Language You'll Hear in Options Trading

Call option – This is basically a contract in which Person A tells Person B that Person B is allowed to buy commodity/stock C at price x, regardless of market price y, as long as Person B exercises their contract by expiration date d.

Put option – The inverse of a call option; Person A tells Person B that Person B is allowed to *sell* commodity/stock C at price x regardless of market price y, as long as Person B exercises their contract by expiration date d.

Derivative – the total value of the security that comes from the purchase amount and the assets that stand underneath the total value of the contract

Expiration date – the point in which the contract will expire, and it will then not be able to make any more money. If a contract holder does not sell the contract before that time, he or she will lose out on the money that was paid for the contract.

Long position – The person who is buying an options contract is in the *long position*. They have the option, though not the obligation, to exercise the contract by a given date.

Options contract – the actual contract that is purchased as an investment. It outlines the price, the value that is going to come and the expiration date of the contract at which point it becomes completely useless to the people who have the contract and who want to be able to sell it.

Reasons for Options Trading

The two biggest reasons that most people use options trading as their main form of investment are speculation and hedging. When it comes to these two particular niches, options fill them out particularly well.

The speculation part is easy. Options trading allows you to essentially bet that stock/commodity c will rise to price y by date d. If you buy the stock/commodity c at price x, and it rises to price y – which just happens to be \$10 more than price x – then you gain a total of \$10 per share/unit in profit, if you turn around and sell the asset/commodity instantly at price y. You get the $10 in profit per share/unit because the options contract allowed you the ability to buy the stock/commodity c at price x even when the actual market price was y. So, with options trading, you can *assume* that an asset or commodity is going to rise in value massively for some reason or another, and then get an options contract *now* letting you buy it at a set price *later*, so that you can turn a profit simply selling the asset or commodity at market price.

Hedging, on the other hand, is one of the lowest risk tactics in options trading. The people who use hedging are able to get more out of the experiences that they have because hedging provides an assurance that their money will be safe. The options that you purchase will only be available so that you can reduce the amount of loss on your investments. If you are going to hedge with options, you need to make sure that you are doing it in combination with other stocks and trading options that you have.

How it All Works

If you have a contract that has different guarantees on it when it comes to finances, you will be able to use that contract to make sure that you are going to get more money from the various assets and commodities that you're working with. The market price of a stock that you have may be at a certain point at any one point in time. Then, the price may go up. Depending on what the options contract was written with, the price will go up with it. The contract is usually worth 100 times the rise in the stock because it is 100 shares worth of that fund.

For example, if you have an options contract that says you have 100 shares of a stock for company X, then when the price of the stock rises for company X, so does the value of your options contract. If company X goes from a value of $10 to $18, then your contract will also go up by eight points. Because you have 100 shares within that contract, it will actually be worth $800 more.

Orders for Options Trading

When you have an options contract, you will need to create some orders that will tell your broker to do specific things. These can be things like stopping the options from losing too much money or simply limiting the amount of money that gets spent on the options. If you know which order you want to use, you will be able to make sure that you are going to truly be able to have your broker do the best work possible.

Limit orders give your broker the price that you will buy or sell for.

Stop limit orders will limit the way that you are able to change your money around between different options trading contracts.

Market orders tell your broker to only act if the options stock is at a specific market price.

Stop market orders do the same as stop loss, but they are based on the market value of the options stock.

Stop loss orders are just like any other type of stop loss. You tell your broker where you want to stop losing money at.

CHAPTER 4: HOW TO GET STARTED WITH OPTIONS TRADING

One of the hardest parts of options trading is actually getting started with it. You will need to take several steps if you want to start trading and each of these steps will require you to do different things. The great part about stock options and options trading is that you will be able to use the previous starting points that you had with options trading if you ever make the decision to start a new type of trade. There are many different things that you can do when getting started out with stock options trading, and it's important that you give all of them ample thought.

Understand Your Goals

You should know what your objectives are before you start options trading. This is to help you have a clear idea of where you want to be when you are getting started, so that you can make sure that you are making all of the right options trading decisions for *you*. It can sometimes be difficult to know what you want to get out of stocks and trading.

Do you want to make a little money on the side? Do you want to replace your full-time income? Are you hoping for passive income?

Each of these things will help you to have a better understanding of the ultimate goal that you have in mind. You need to make sure that you are on the right path to get that which you want when you are looking at the different paths within an options trading career.

Try Strategies

There are several different strategies that will help you to have a better understanding of the way that options trading works. Following these strategies can be complicated at worst and stupidly simple at best. The majority of the strategies that people use for options trading are outlined in this book so that you can follow them and make sure that you are getting the best experience possible with trading.

Choose the one that best lines up with your capabilities and with the end goal that you have for your trading. If you know what you want to do with options trading and if you work to always make sure that you are getting to that point, it will be much easier for you to figure out the specific steps that you need to take while you are trading.

Always Use a Broker

Having a broker is one of the only ways to ensure that you will be able to be successful with options trading. A broker can not only help you get the best advice that you need for trades, but he or she will also help you to figure out where you need to go with each of the trades that you have. It is a good idea to try different things that the broker suggests and to make sure that you are going to be able to use these options when it comes time to trade. There are many different aspects of trading so be sure that you are paying attention to all of them.

The broker will not only be able to help you figure out what you need to do with trades and with the options contracts that you have but will also be able to help you figure out if you meet the requirements for being able to get involved in options trading.

Can You Participate?

There is a chance that you may not be eligible for options trading. About 30% of people who have the goal of options trading are not actually able to do the trades that they want to do. There are different factors that go into determining your eligibility, but the majority of them have to do with risk. If you are deemed to be high risk, if your portfolio is not large enough to satisfy the requirements, or if you show that you are somehow not able to fit options trading into your portfolio in a way that makes sense, you will not be able to participate in options trading.

Just like with other parts of trading, things can always change, though. Keep that in mind when you make the decision to try new things with options trading. You will be able to try new things, and you can even change your eligibility with time. Eligibility for options trading, indeed, is something that everyone can work toward.

Before you make the decision to invest in options trading, always check with your broker to make sure that you are eligible to do it.

The Trading Account

Once you have determined whether or not you are eligible for options trading, you will then be able to start your trading account. This is generally different from a traditional trade account in that it is a margin account. You can make sure that you are doing everything right with options contracts by starting up the margin account before you put the money into the stocks. It is a good idea to know what kind of account you are going to have and what the initial investment is going to look like for you when you start out with any sort of trading.

If you do not already have a margin account, you will need to talk to your broker about it. This is where all of the options trading actions will occur so you need to make sure that you are making a worthwhile decision about your trading account. This will essentially serve to make sure you're getting the most bang for your buck. You can also make sure that you are getting the best experience possible when your broker starts your margin account with you.

CHAPTER 5: THE DIFFERENT TYPES OF STOCK OPTIONS

There are different types of options contracts that you can choose from when you are getting started. The type of option contract that will work best for you will depend on the total capital that you have to put into the account along with the risk that you may carry. There are different things that you can choose from, and you should make sure that the options contracts that you act on line up with your goals.

Overview of Options

Options contracts largely depend upon the volatility of a stock and the amount of money which is invested. It is important to note that all of the different types of stock options can be deducted from that first initial capital function. It is a good idea to recognize that you will be able to put more money into the options stocks that you have within the contracts, but you will never have the option to lower your initial investment amount. You can always invest more but you can never uninvest without taking a potential loss.

Buying or Selling

When you are looking at the options contract that you have, it will be clear to see whether or not you are the buyer or seller. Your position will be outlined, and you will be able to figure out what the difference is between the two different parties. In each of the contracts that you have, you can only be the buyer or the seller.

For example, if you are the buyer of one contract, you will not have the opportunity to be the seller of that same contract. Instead, when you are ready to sell – and not just buy - options, you will need to make the decision to set up new contracts with assets that you already *own* (or intend to own). You can always ask your broker for assistance, here.

Striking Price

In the contract, the price is listed. The strike price is the point at which you can buy the option that is listed in the contract. It is important to note that you will not be able to buy before it reaches that price. Period.

If you are a buyer on the contract, you will also have a strike price at which you can sell. This tells you that you cannot sell until it hits the strike price. It is clear to see that this is much different from what is offered with futures. When there is a future, there is no specific strike price, but there is a strike date. The seller cannot sell before it reaches that point on the calendar. With options, you can still sell before it reaches any type of date (and you *should* sell before it hits the expiration, certainly) but you need to just be sure that it is at the right price.

The Expiration

Every single options contract will have an expiration date. This is something that must be closely monitored. For this reason, you are advised to have a broker. The broker will be able to tell you what you are doing and when the expiration date is approaching. If you find that you are getting close to the expiration date, you need to sell off the option even if your profit is not as high as what you would like it to be. If you don't, you'll lose the money that you initially put into the investment, and that can be a terrible way to start out with options trading.

Premium Investment

Your premium is basically the same as any other type of premium that you would see in investing and in stocks. It is the amount of money that you paid to purchase the options contract.

Make sure that your premium is enough to purchase the options contract but is not so much that you are going to lose a large amount of money on the trades that you are doing. You should always be careful with the stocks that you have,but options are a whole other ballpark of carefulness. Since they are somewhat of a risk, you definitely want to go for one that has a lower premium. If you do this, you will put yourself as a lower risk investment which will not only help you to lose less money but will also make you have a better appearance with your portfolio.

Style of Option

There are two main styles of options stocks.

American style – you can use the rights that you have in your contract at anytime that you have the contract in your possession. You do not have to wait until the actual expiration date so that you have more time to keep yourself from losing money. You can sell at any time after the price has hit the strike out amount.

European style – you are required to wait until the actual expiration date to be able to use that selling option. This can be a problem because it is sometimes difficult to sell a stock in one day. For example, you cannot sell the stock until you have reached the expiration date, but if you go for longer than the expiration date, you will lose out on the money that you have in your stock option contract. This is detrimental because you will not have that money that you put into the premium of the contract, so you will start out with a loss.

While the American option is the more popular among people who are trading, it is something that you will need to decide for yourself. Other than the expiration date specifics of each style, there are no major differences between the two styles of option contracts.

CHAPTER 6: CHOOSING INDEX OPTIONS

The Index Options are slightly different types of contracts, and working with them can drastically change the way that you are working with options contracts. They are simply another style that you can use when you are trading and when you have the different aspects of your trades lined up. When you choose to use an index option stock, you are simply choosing a different way that you can invest your money in the stocks that you think will be profitable.

Indexes

The most common type of index options that are available is the DJIA and the NASDAQ, which are both included in different sectors. The Dow Jones is included with companies that have very large caps on them. The initial investments, or premiums, are usually much higher with the DJIA. With the NASDAQ, you will be getting an investment that is closer to the technological side of investing, but it will cost you much less money than if you were doing it in any other way.

Choices

You can choose any sector within the two major types of indexes. This will allow you the chance to make sure that you are going to be able to get the different benefits that come with the sectors. If you are particularly interested in a sector or if you find that it is one that seems to do well according to the research that you have done, you should make that choice. It can sometimes be difficult to decide what you have done and what you are going to do in the future. If you do not know what choice you are going to make, it is wise to check with your broker. While the broker will not be able to tell you which decision you should make, he or she can give you the various beneficial points that come with each of the investments.

Advantages

The best part about the index options is that you will be able to profit in several different sectors when it comes to investing. You can get your hands into the business of many different types of investments, and that will help you to get exactly what you need with your investing opportunities. You will also be able to make more money.

The more streams of income that you have that come from investing in general, the more you will be able to profit and the more you will be able to benefit from all of the different stock price increases.

If you are going to use index options for stocks, you should make sure that you are trying more than one sector. Doing this will enable you to truly get an understanding how each of the sectors works, as well as giving you the added perk of diversified investments.

Settlement

The cash that comes from index options is the settlement amount. Since you are not actually purchasing money or investing cash in the way that you would with traditional investments, you will need to make sure that you are converting your indexes into cash. While this can sometimes be difficult to do, you need to make sure that it is something that you are prepared for. The difference in the values of the index is calculated by using the strike price. What is leftover from the strike price is what you will collect on in cash. That is what your return will be.

Capping Index

The capped index options are available to people who have options contracts. They were created so that the index option can be sold off as soon as it reaches the cap. There is no other type of trading option that gives you this type of choice. When you are making the decision to invest in options stocks, you will need to determine whether or not you want to take advantage of the capped index options and whether or not that is going to be worth the extra amount that you need to do to get to that point.

Risk Leverage

When you are looking at the risks that are associated with Options contracts and the index style of these stocks, you will need to figure out which ones are the riskiest and which ones are going to bring a low risk to you. Of course, the lower that you put the premium, the lower the risk is going to be for the stock options so you should always keep that in mind when you are looking at stock options and at the different aspects that come with them. Be sure that you are always leveraging the risks that are associated with the trades so that you can make sure that you are putting all of the options that you have in your trading portfolio.

Multiplied Contracts

When you are choosing your index options, you can get a contract multiplier. This is something that will allow you the chance to cash out on the value of the index and of the options contract that is included with the index. Make sure that you are using the options contracts that you have to be able to get the best experience possible for your trade options. Always work to provide yourself with the best trades for your portfolio and for the different things that you are adding to it.

The Premium

As with traditional options stocks, you will need to pay the premium with cash. It's sad, but true; paying premiums is an absolutely necessary part of working with options. If you are using cash for your premium, you will then be able to get the multiplier and cash in on the amount that the options stock has built up for you over the period of time that you have had it in your portfolio.

CHAPTER 7: CHOOSING CURRENCY OPTIONS

There are different trade options that will make a difference depending on the type of trade that you are doing. With options stocks, you can choose to use the index option, which is beneficial to people who do not want to deal in currency. The other option that is available, though, is currency. This is where you invest your money into the options stocks, and they are able to use the different types of currency within their own functions. This is something that is necessary if you want to be able to get the best experience possible and if you want to make sure that you are going to get your full investment back – and hopefully more.

While there are no multipliers with this type of options trade, there are different benefits that will help you to get back more cash when it comes to your trading. You do not have to worry about how much the trade value is going to change because the index does not play a part in this. You will simply have to worry about whether or not the currency that is present in these situations is fluctuating. If it is not, you can just collect on the amount that you initially put in as the financial premium.

The forex (Foreign Exchange) options provide a tool that traders and investors who are in the options contract trading business can use to make profit. They do not have to purchase the actual currency to be able to get to this point and simply have to use the leverage that they have within their portfolios so that they can make sure that they are getting the most out of the trading options available to them.

The contracts can be held when there is a currency options trade going on. This will help to reduce the amount of risk that occurs from trading and will help to prove that there will be profits from the different options that are included in all of the trades. When looking at trades, brokers and investors will both be able to see that a held contract is always a good way to reduce risk.

Choosing a currency option stock will always be lower risk than an index stock, but the payouts are often also much lower when you are using the currency trade models.

If you are using the forex model for your currency options trading portfolio, you will need to make sure that you are doing it the right way. There are different options when it comes to each of these, but they all involve the use of the forex system. If you do not want to use theforex, you will need to find a broker who does not participate in it. Brokers are not able to do forex options in addition to forex trading, because of the implications that come along with it. Investors, though, are actually able to choose two different brokers who do these things.

While there are regulations on the brokers and how they each can do the different things with the trading, there are very few on the investors when it comes to currency options trading. This is necessary for people who want to make sure that they are going to be able to get the most money possible from the trades that they are doing. It is also something that can help investors to realize what they are doing with the different trading options.

SPOT

The SPOT style of trading is intended for people who have a huge amount of startup capital they can use in order to get into forex trading. It is a high investment option and is generally not recommended for beginners, but some who have chosen it as their first options trading stock have done well with it. If you have the right broker who is able to use your stops and calls in the way that you want, you will be able to get a much better outcome from the SPOT trading option.

When you do Single Payment Options Trading, or SPOT, you will be able to bring about the different trading options. SPOT is created to automatically help you get the trades that you want. You can set up everything before you start trading and it will help you to get the payout options that you want. It will also give you the chance to be able to include all of the different aspects of trading. With SPOT, you will get a payment each time that you have made a prediction on the options trade and you are right. For those who are confident in their prediction skills, it can actually be worth the higher investment.

Call Options

The calling options that are included with the different forex styles operate almost identically to index options trading, but they are different in the sense that they involve real cash and currency that is going to change depending on the market and what is going on with the various businesses. If you know what you are doing, you will be able to call out the options and the information that is contained with each of them.

As you learn more about the call options and about the different things that are associated with the call options, you will be able to adjust the different types of options to your calling point. It is always a good idea to include the different things that are reduced with calling and putting the information into the algorithms. As you are learning more about the way that things are done in trading, the chances are that you will want to switch from this type of forex trade to one that allows you to get a single payment.

While call options are great for people who are just getting started in options trading, most usually move onto the SPOT model where they can get higher payouts for a slightly higher risk.

CHAPTER 8: ETF AND THE FUTURE OPTIONS

Just because options trading is slightly different from future trading does not necessarily mean that you can avoid everything about futures trading. It can sometimes be difficult to figure out exactly what you need to do to make sure that you are going to get each of the different options contracts to go your way; knowing more about everything related to options can help with this, including futures.

As you are looking at the options stocks, you should also consider the ETF, or exchange traded funds, along with the future options so that you can make sure that you are getting the best deal possible.

Exchange traded funds are the mutual funds of the options trading world. They are handled just like mutual funds, and they can be traded like stocks and shares are traditionally traded. If you are working with the different types of ETFs, you can look at them in the same way as mutual funds and trades.

You do not need to have a special margin account to be able to use ETFS. This is because they are available and it is legal to trade them on the regular stock exchange. You don't have to worry about the way that they are being traded or any of the implications that come along with using a smaller account or a margin account that could bring about problems in your portfolio. Always make sure that you are working with your ETFs in the same way that you would work with traditional stocks and shares.

Diversity

When you are using options trading, ETF is one of the best chances at gaining diversity in your portfolio. Since they can be traded on the open stock market, they are simple to add to your portfolio, and they can make a huge difference in the way that your portfolio looks. Always make sure that you are trying new things and that you are working to promote the different aspects of your portfolio. With ETF, you can see that there is a major difference in the way that stocks are traded in the field.

Larger Volumes

ETFs are also great if you want to have a large volume of stocks. They can be purchased in mass quantities, but the prices are generally close to the same of what a similar stock would cost you on the open market. Since they are slightly more complex than a traditional stock, they will eventually grow to be worth more than what the stocks are. This will give you the chance to see that they can be traded and they will be able to be purchased for different amounts. It is always a good idea to try out different stocks and to make sure that you have things like ETFs available in your trading portfolio so that you don't have to worry about the implications that come along with not having a diversified portfolio.

Risks

Perhaps one of the biggest benefits that come with ETFs is also their downfall. Since they are so complex, it is important to note that they cannot be used in the way that other stocks are able to be used. You must make sure that you are diversifying your portfolio heavily. Since you have them in there, you need to trade them.

If you have never had a complex stock like an ETF, you will want to check with your broker for advice on what can be done with the stock and the way that you can work to make sure that the stock is truly working for you.

Futures

Despite the fact that futures were the forerunner for options trading, they have not become completely obsolete just because options are now more prominent. In fact, there is actually a chance that futures have grown in popularity as a result of options trading. If you are hoping to diversify your portfolio even further, consider futures but also consider the implications that come with future trading options.

The Stock Exchange with Futures

Similar to options trading, you need to make sure that you have a specific margin account that was designed to be used with futures. This will help prevent you from running into major problems that could happen in the Open Stock Exchange. You cannot use futures on the stock exchange, and they will be separate from it despite the fact that the returns will be determined based on the stock exchange. Try to find the best margin fund for your futures so that you can have them separate from your options trading.

Pricing

The premium that you would typically see with a future is usually about the same as what you would see with options stocks. This is because they are very similar. Where you must wait for the date with futures, you must wait for the price with options stocks. It is a good idea to always try and make sure that you are dividing your investments evenly between the two so that, if you lose out on one, you will still have a chance to profit on the other.

Strike Dates

There is no expiration date on the futures. This is because they are meant to go infinitely unlike the options trading. There is, however, a price that you must reach before you can buy or sell the contract. That is the downside to the trades and is something that propelled the reasoning behind the options trading. It is important to know that you cannot sell unless you are at that price. You must also be able to reach a future date before you can sell. Without the expiration date, you don't have to be in such a hurry to sell, but you *do* have to wait a specified amount of time.

CHAPTER 9: OPTIONS TRADING STRATEGY TERMS

You should never jump into options trading without knowing the implications of it and the various things that you can do to make the trades better. You need to know the strategies that are available to traders, if you want to ever have a chance at making things work out within your trade portfolio. It can be easy to get caught up in the problems that come along with options trading, so make sure that you are always following the prescribed strategies so that you do not miss out on the money that you *could* be making from each of the trades.

To get the best advice on the strategies, you will need to know the terms that are used.

Bull – investor who wants to make the market asset increase. It is someone who buys up the assets and then sells them once it increases. Functions as a traditional type of investor.

Bull spread – when the bulls work to make sure that they are able to get the different things that they want in the options trading. They will often buy up several different trade options, and then they will sell them quickly. They operate as professionals and are often able to predict when there is going to be a change in the market.

Bear – completely opposite from bulls. They look for decreases in the market, and they sell off their options trades in anticipation of the drop in the price. They will then repurchase them at the lower price later on when the prices do go down.

Bear spread – the same thing as a bull spread but opposite on the level that they sell and re-buy the trades that they have worked with before.

Downside – when the hedging tool helps you to limit the loss that you have on your assets. It is often used in combination with options contracts so that you can make sure that you are getting the most out of the other types of investments that you have in your own portfolio.

Vertical – the investor wants to sell and buy at the same time. This usually does not happen exactly at the same time, but it is within a few seconds of the happening that comes along with the trades. It is necessary for investors to make sure that they are losing out on the bad deals and gaining profits on the good options trades.

Collar – another type of protection that will work similarly to hedging and will provide the investor with the security that they need when there is a huge dip in the stock market. By putting a money option into the options trade and then writing the option as if he or she were out of money, they can make sure that they are using the collar to protect themselves.

Straddle – when an investor is riding both of the options that they have. They can actually do this with more than one option, but it is usually difficult to do so especially for investors who are just starting out. They must then make a decision which one they are going to jump on and take the investment opportunity with.

Strangle – the way the investor is able to work with two completely different types of investments. The investor will do all of these different things at the same time, and the intent is for the option contracts to increase in value. Investors should know which direction each of the options are going and they should be confident in the fact that they are doing different things. If an investor does not know the direction that the investment is going in, there are implications that can often cause the investor to lose the money that they have put into the options trades.

Butterfly trading – this is similar to a vertical trade, but it is different in that itis on a much larger scale. It involves using several different options trades and making sure that they are being simultaneously sold and purchased at the same time. An investor will do this if he or she thinks that there is going to be a big change in the market. By selling and buying at the same time, he will set himself up for the changes that are going to come in the market, and it will make things much easier when the change *does* happen to the market – whether it is a drop or a rise in the price.

If you are able to look at each of these terms and know what they mean in a grander sense, you are then ready to move onto the next chapter. If you feel that you are still not familiar with them, study them and apply them to real world situations.

The easiest way to practice the terms, learn what they mean, who they apply to, and the way that you can use them on your own is to create a practice scenario. Figure out the trading scenario that you want to come up with and label each of the parts of it. If you are confident with your trading terms, you should then try to learn the different aspects of the trades and what they will mean to you.

It is always a good idea to make sure that you are familiar with the basic terminology because that is just the starting point.

While these terms are helpful and they can create a better outlook for you while you are investing, you will be able to learn much more when you start the true trading process. You will quickly find that these are just a starting point and that there are so many more points that you will need to keep track of when you are doing different things in the trading field. Always learn as much as you can and make note of it. Consider

keeping these terms handy so that you
can use them later on.

CHAPTER 10: THE OPTIONS TRADING STRATEGY

Learning the different types of strategies that are available to you will help you to make the right choice when it comes time for you to start trading and getting the profits that you desire from the trades that you make. It is a good idea to be sure that you know which strategy is going to work for you based on the goals that you have set up for yourself. When you are working to make sure that you are choosing the right type of strategy, you can figure out which options line up with the goals that you have and how you want to involve all of the different aspects.

Long Position

People who want to buy a lot before the price increases generally use this type of strategy. If you want to create a large profit over a long period of time, you can take advantage of having a long position available to you.

Since you can base your position off of the leverage that you are going to get from the trading options, you will be able to use the leverage to your advantage. If you have a very strong portfolio, the long position will work the best with you.

If you are going to invest your money, consider doing so with the $5,000 model in the shares that you are going to use. If the average price of the shares is $127, you can get 39 shares out of the company. If you want to add just a bit more money, you can get the full 40 shares out of the company. If the shares go up over the period of time that you have them in, your shares' value will go up, too. When you are investing in the shares, you need to keep in mind that it sometimes takes a long time to get a return on the shares. In the short time that the shares went up by just a few dollars, you would have profited only around $120. If you wait just a little longer, the shares will probably rise again, and you will be able to profit even more from the initial investment that you made. The long position takes patience and time, but it is often worth it if you want to get the highest profits possible.

Short Position

You can purchase the stocks for a short position if you do not want to risk a lot of money. Wait until the price goes way down before you buy them and then allow yourself the chance to purchase them at a low price. Before they drop again, sell them. This would make you a bearish type of trader in a market that is bullish. You can try different things with short positioning, but you will almost always profit more if you can sellthe shares for a profit quicker. After you have sold them (before the decrease), you should wait until the decrease happens. When it does, use the profit that you received from selling them and then buy them back up again. Do this over and over again until the market stops decreasing.

Most of the people who are taking options trading approaches for the first time will generally use this type of strategy. It is safer than long positioning, it brings profits in right away, and it makes it easier for people to be sure that they are going to get the best return possible for the trades that they have. It is also something that will show you how much money you *can* make from options trading so that it will give you a boost at the beginning.

Calling Covers

If you combine the short and the long positions together, you will get the strategy that most people use once they are comfortable with both short and long. You should first learn the short position. Next, take a bull approach and try to use the long position. From there, you can combine them both. Buy stocks when they are very low and hang onto them until they are very high. Sell them off before the decrease and then repurchase them so that you can make sure that you are making money when they are at the lowest amount possible. If you want to be able to get the best experience possible with your trading, you will be able to learn both short and long positioning.

There is not a single investor out there who is successful and who only uses either short or long positioning. All of the best investors will be able to use both of them in combination with each other so that they can make sure that they are getting the best experience possible. It is necessary for investors to make sure that they are going to be able to do everything that they can when it comes to their position.

Protection

There are times when you may come across options trades that seem like they are going to be risky. You may see that their returns are going to be great but the initial investment is very risky and something that you will have to weigh against the potential benefits. If you go for this risky sort of investment, consider the protection that comes with it.

Similar to how you use options stocks to create a hedge for your traditional trading, you can also use hedges for the options stocks. This will help you to make sure that you are protected and that you are going to be able to be as protected as possible from any negative ramifications. You can be unafraid to take risks that are associated with trading when you know that you have a hedge in place that can protect you. Be sure that you do this when you know that the rewards are going to be better than what some of the risks are. Your financial protective structures will help to balance the weight with the problems.

CHAPTER 11: ENSURING SUCCESS WITH OPTIONS TRADING

There is no way to guarantee that you are going to be successful 100% of the time with any type of trading, especially options trading. The idea behind options trading is that it is slightly riskier than any other type of trading, but on the other hand, if you do it the right way, you will witness some of the largest returns you will ever see across any form of trading. The general idea in the world of finance is that the amount of risk is correlative to the amount of reward. This is true even with options trading. It may be hard to figure out the right way to do it but following each of these tips will guarantee that you have given yourself a chance to make money from the trades that you have initiated.

Build Capital

Before you start investing in any way, you need to build up capital. You cannot expect to have good returns on an investment if it is just a small amount. While you may be very proud of yourself for having 100 dollars in your bank account, the bad news is that this is just not enough to get started with investing. If you want to be able to even come close to purchasing worthwhile options contracts, you will need far above $1,000 to get started. You can get cheaper ones... but the thing is that those contracts are cheap for a reason.

Keep saving, and you will, eventually, have the money that you need to invest. By the way, are you using a high-interest savings account to save that money? You should be!

Wise Investment

No matter what type of options trade you are going to get involved in, you need to make sure that the investment is one that makes sense. Do all of the required research on the company before you invest your money into it. If you don't do this, you will risk not getting the return that you want from the investment. An investment is an *investment*. Why would you invest into something that you know nothing about? You will probably struggle at first when it comes to all of the different aspects of options trading, and you may find starting out that it's even a bit overwhelming. However, always try your best and keep a close eye on the different market approaches to trading. Wisdom comes solely from experience.

Take (Some) Risks

There are always going to be risks with trading. Whether they are risks dealing directly with your capital supply or risks dealing more specifically with your different investitures is dependent upon how good of a trader you are. Be sure that you work hard to take the right kind of risks and that you are taking the right kind of chances. You should learn what you are comfortable with when it comes to the risks that you are going to take. How much do the benefits outweigh the risk? Is the benefit big enough that it will be worth it if you lose the money that you put into the investment? If your answer is no, you probably should not take the risk.

Adjust Your Positioning

If you find that you are struggling to get the positioning right with your investment, you should change it. This does not mean that you will make a huge switch from a long position to a short position or the other way around, but it does mean that you will need to make sure that you are going to get the best return possible from wherever you are. Take specific and special pains to write down how you are performing from both the short and long positions. Consider the results. Do you consistently perform badly in the long position? Look at what's happening in those trades – every aspect – and see where things are going wrong. In the end, if you are finding that your position isn't working, just try your best to change it and to make sure that you will be able to include different options with the positions that you initially set out to take.

Re-Invest the Money

When you make money, you need to reinvest that money. With the money just sitting there, you are not going to be able to earn more on it. Since you have the money in the first place, take the smallest amount of profit off of it to pay yourself and then reinvest the rest of the money so that you can, quite simply, use your profits in order to turn more profits.

Broker Experience

When you are shopping for a broker, make sure that the broker who you are going to work with has experience in options trading. There may be brokers who have years of experience on the open stock exchange, but they may not have any idea about the options trading sector. This can mean different things for different people, but it is always a good idea to make sure that you get pertinent and up-to-date information from your broker. If your broker *does* have experience with options trading, make sure that it is the kind of experience that you are looking for and that it is something that you can use to make your trading options more professional. This is especially important if you have never traded before and if you want to get the best trading profits possible. Does your broker have a positive history with the options trading sector? Do what you can to find out.

Don't Put All Your Eggs In One Basket

Make sure that you are trying different types of options trades. If you have a lot of money to invest, don't invest it all in one type of options trading. Instead, invest it in several different options contracts that seem like they would be a good fit for your portfolio. Always do your best to ensure that you are choosing *good* options contracts and that the trades that you have are ones that will make the most sense for you and your portfolio.

Consider the Payout

You need to keep the end game in mind each time that you try to invest in different things. The end game, of course, is the payout that you are going to be able to get when you exercise an options contract. If you are looking for different options that are within your trading budget, you will need to make sure that you are doing everything that you can to include these new potential option contracts.

Try Something New

Trying new things is a great way to ensure that you are going to be able to get the highest profit possible. If you are not aware of the different profits that come from different trade options, you – quite simply – are just going to remain inexperienced and won't ever become a masterful options trader. Each time that you decide to invest again, take a look around. Take into account all of the information available to you about every single stock on the various markets that you're looking at.

CHAPTER 12: IS PASSIVE INCOME POSSIBLE WITH OPTIONS TRADING?

Many people look for passive income. They put a lot of work into their trading in the beginning so that they do not have to do as much later on and so that they can make sure that they are going to continue profiting for years to come. What most people don't know, though, is that it is actually difficult to gain passive income from things like options investing.

Set It Up

You can prepare for passive income by always setting up your options trading with the things that you want it to do. You should have a good idea of the way that it works and the different things that you can do with options trading before you try to step back and away from the different things that happen in trading. You can expect to be options trading for at least five years before you know the different things that will set you up for passive income success. When you have done this, and you are constantly recycling the money that you have made back into the investments, you will know that you are ready to try to make passive income.

You Need a Broker

While you should have a broker who is helping you with your options trading already, you will need a broker who will be able to help you run the whole operation. This can be the regular broker that you have been using the whole time or it can be someone new who specializes in the type of passive income that you want to be able to make. If you find a good broker who is also able to help you with your passive income goals, you should rely on that one to do it for you when you try to make passive income.

Automation

There are certain things that you can use in order to automate the trading process. This will not work all of the time if you are doing options trading, but you can make sure that you have certain safeguards in place that will allow you to make passive income. The whole process cannot be completely automated – that's what your broker is for – but automation *is* something that will take a lot of the pressure off of the whole affair of options trading. Computers are, in some ways, smarter than people. They can be programmed to make the best decisions and every computer error is simply a human error coming back down the line.

Use Stops

Stop losses, limits, and protocols can all be put in place to ensure that you don't lose *too* much money. This means that you will need to figure out the right way to do each of these things and that you will need to include all of these different things with your assets and options trading. Always make sure that your broker knows where you want to stop the loss or limit the trades at so that you don't lose all of the money that you have built up in the time leading up to when you started to take a more hands-off approach to the deals.

In closing, yes, you can make passive income with options trading. It is not easy, though, so you may want to just keep doing options trading on your own and profiting off of it in that way. If you'd like to make passive income off of it though, it is most certainly possible. You need a very good and competent broker behind you, too.

CONCLUSION

Thank for making it through to the end
of *A Beginner's Guide to Options
Trading.* Let's hope it was informative
and able to provide you with all of the
tools you need to achieve your goals of
making money through the various
options trading sectors.

The next step is to start saving up your
money or to head out on your search for

the perfect broker who will help you learn as much as you can about the trades that will one day make you rich.

OPTIONS TRADING:THE ULTIMATE GUIDE TO OPTIONS TRADING UNCOVERING OPTIONS TRADING PROFIT MAKING SECRETS

DESCRIPTION

If you have ever spent any real time trading in one or more of the asset investment markets, then you know how little freedom you sometimes have to go your own way and set your parameters for financial success as they make sense to you. Not so with options trading, which, as the name implies provides you with the option, not the obligation to carry through on what you have started. What's more based on the state of the market at the moment, you can easily transfer all of your existing skill into this new way of trading without missing a beat. If you are already somewhat familiar with options trading but want to take your skills to the next level then

Options Trading: The Ultimate Guide to Options Trading is the book you have been waiting for.

Studies show that barely more than 10 percent of all options traders display the type of mindset that will help them be successful in the long term. Inside you will learn not just what it takes to form the type of mindset that will lead you to success, you will also learn important tips that the best options traders utilize on a daily basis along with the mistakes that many traders of all skill levels fall into and how you can avoid them for yourself. You will also learn what a reliable options trading plan looks like and how to measure the metrics of your current system to ensure that it measures up.

When it comes to being successful in the options trading market, it is all about the strategies that you use which is why inside you will find more than a dozen different strategies that are proven effective. You will find strategies that you will use every day as well as those which are going to be useful in more specialized situations. No matter your skill level or experience, *Options Trading: The Ultimate Guide to Options Trading* has something you can use.

If you know that you have it in you to be successful in the asset market, but you haven't quite found the right niche, then what are you waiting for? Take control of your financial future and buy this book today!

Inside you will find

- The difference between liquid and illiquid options and which you stay away from more often than not.

- Why it is important to consider historical volatility before you make any moves.

- Which metrics you are going to want to consider in order to determine if your trading plan is a dud or a financial stud.

- Ten different trading strategies for all seasons and market moods and how to get the most out of each one.

- Several specialized and advanced trading techniques and when to use them for maximum profit.

- *And more...*

INTRODUCTION

Congratulations on downloading *Options Trading: The Ultimate Guide to Options Trading* and thank you for doing so. When it comes to jumping into investment trading, options are easier than many other choices only because they rely more on existing knowledge of the underlying asset markets. This doesn't mean it is a straightforward process, however, and if you aren't careful, you can lose the sum total of your trading capital just as quickly as anywhere else.

To help ensure you are as successful as possible, the following chapters will discuss everything you need to know in order to ensure your time spent trading options is as easy and fruitful as possible. First, you will learn all about the mindset you need to adopt if you are going to be successful at options trading, not just in the short term but for the long term as well. From there you will learn many of the essential tips for success that experienced options traders use every day as well as the mistakes that many traders of all skill levels fall into and how you can avoid them for yourself. You will also learn about the importance of analyzing your trades and how to make sure that your trading system or plan is as efficient as possible. Finally, you will learn all about the many different trading strategies that you will use on a regular basis as well as several more specific trading strategies that can lead to major profits if utilized successfully. When you are finished there will be no option, no matter how convoluted that can stand in your way.

There are plenty of books on this subject on the market, thanks again for choosing this one! Every effort was made to ensure it is full of as much useful information as possible, please enjoy!

CHAPTER 1: THE MINDSET OF THE SUCCESSFUL OPTIONS TRADER

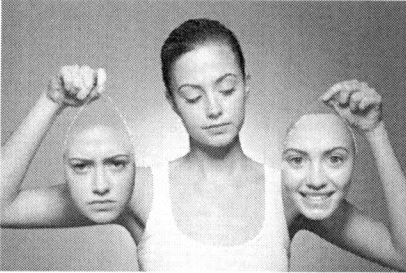

Studies show that barely more than 10 percent of all options traders display the type of mindset that will help them be successful in the long term. If you ever hope to be one of them, the first thing you need to do is to separate your emotions from your actions. Instead of letting your emotions factor into your trading strategy you need to remove them from the equation entirely by striving for the purely logical mindset that the best options traders cultivate. Following the suggestions outlined below will allow you to focus on long-term success regardless of what distractions are currently taking place around you, naturally improve your successful trade ratio in the process.

Have the right expectations: When it comes to honing your trader's mindset, perhaps the most important thing you can do is understand the results you are likely to experience. Having realistic expectations will allow you to respond appropriately both in times of failure as well as success. Specifically, this means you are going to want to banish thoughts of major success in a short period of time. This, in turn, will make it easier for you to prevent negative thoughts from creeping in throughout the day and causing you to take risks you otherwise would not take.

Additionally, it is important to be aware of what your emotional triggers are while trading. As everyone's triggers are different, the best way to understand your own is to keep a trading journal. In this journal, you are going to want to keep track of all of your trades, both successful and unsuccessful. You are going to want to note the date of each trade, the specifics surrounding it, the emotions you felt at the time, whether or not it was successful and why.

This exercise will not only help you to be aware of the emotions you are likely to experience in the future; it will help you understand why they appear in the first place. Emotions are the enemy of good trades and the best way to outpace your enemy is to know them inside and out.

For many traders, the strongest emotional triggers occur because they believe that correctly executing on a plan should lead to success 100 percent of the time. This stems from a misunderstanding of what considering a plan successful actually means. When it comes to options trading, a successful plan is one that hovers around a 60 percent success rate. This means that the scheme is extremely likely to turn a profit in the long run but a full 40 percent of the time it is used it will end in failure.

Losses are an unavoidable part of the investment process as risk is what ultimately leads to profit. If every investment were a guaranteed success, no one would bet against it, and there would be no chance for a profit. To mitigate these feelings, it is important to understand that a good trade is not one that made money but rather one that followed your system to the letter. In order to do so properly, you need to focus exclusively on your long-term results and treat everything else as meaningless noise.

This means you will want to wait at least a month between periods where you update your plan as anything less isn't going to provide you with enough details to make changes effectively. A significant moment in your evolution as an options trader will be the moment you can see why the trader who struck it rich after a few random trades is less successful than a trader with a few different plans that are always executed on properly no matter what. Remember, an effective trader is a selective trader.

Additionally, it is important to view options trading as a marathon rather than a sprint. With this fact in mind, it will be much easier for you to consider unsuccessful trades as a learning experience rather than an abject failure. This will then make it easier to keep emotions out of the equation, a feat that will become even easier with practice.

Understand that sometimes it is okay to do nothing: Another negative mindset that many traders foster hinges on the idea that they always need to be trading. The reality is that inaction can be just as profitable as an extended trading day if the conditions are right. As long as you are not the writer of an option then creating a pull or call doesn't force you to take any specific action if things don't work out in your favor. This fact may seem obvious, but when thought about logically, it becomes difficult to put theory into practice when there is money on the line.

This is why it is important to include situations where not going through with a trade is the right choice in the system that you decide to use. Once again, as long as you listen to the system that you created when your mindset was at its best you have the potential to become an expert options trader.

One of the most important things you need to wean out of your trading habits is jumping into trades without thinking them through entirely. Getting into the habit of picking and choosing the best trades for your system will help you become a professional when it comes to separating the wheat from the chaff. Knowing how to do this will contribute to ensuring that you are not just getting lucky now and then when it comes to making trades.

The same goes for getting out of a trade that turned sour as sticking with it and hoping things turn around is on of the easiest ways to lose your shirt. The best choice is always going to be letting the trade in question speak for itself and, if the trade doesn't go the way you expect, use that as an opportunity to learn for next time.

Put more value on patience: Patience is one of the most important, and most difficult, thing for many traders to learn. This is because sitting idly by with money on the table is such a difficult skill to master. Luckily, like all skills, it can be improved with practice. In order to perfect this skill, it is important to internalize the fact that the market isn't always making big moves, even at times of peak volatility. A useful way of helping yourself learn patience is by never focusing on just one trade at a time. Keeping your options open makes it easier to put each trade in perspective and prevent any one trade from artificially inflating its importance in your mind.

This is not to say that individual trades should be treated flippantly. Rather, you need to consider each trade in a perspective that takes the entirety of your goal into account. Additionally, this means that you are going to want to come to terms with the fact that there will be some days where there just isn't much going on. Overtrading can be just as damaging to your bottom line as not trading enough or making bad trades, especially if your transaction fees are higher than you might prefer.

To help cultivate the right mindset you are going to want to set either monthly or weekly profit goals as opposed to daily trading goals. Setting daily goals will likely cause you to make erratic trades at the end of the day as you strive to meet your goal. Even if you do end up making the target amount each day to hit your goal, it is likely that at least some of these trades will not have stood up to the strict level of scrutiny that a good plan requires. What's worse, if you end up seeing results based on the poorly thought out trades then it can promote the formation of destructive habits moving forward.

It is important to focus on building the type of discipline that will serve you well in the long term as early in your trading career as possible as you will less be less likely to have major trades on the line. The longer you go without giving into your impulses, the easier it will be to ignore them completely.

Learn to adapt: While it is important to stick to your system when your emotions are telling you otherwise, it is equally important to understand that sometimes market situations will change on the fly. When this occurs, you are going to need to go off the book if you hope to see your current trade end in profit. At first, it is going to be difficult to determine when it is the right time to toe the line and when it is the right time to experiment as the only clear indicator is practice.

In order to ensure that you have to fly blind as infrequently as possible, you are going to want to have several different trading plans on hand that is ideal for different market states. Learning which plan is right for which situation and when it is time for a change, in real time, will help you see much greater overall returns a much greater portion of the time.

Regardless of your planning, sometimes the unexpected will occur which means that you will need to make a leap of faith in order to be successful. A competent trader will be aware of market signs that change is on the horizon and will be able to act accordingly. This is another skill that cannot be taught; it can only be gained by experience.

As long as you keep the appropriate mindset regarding individual trades, any new strategy that is attempted will result in valuable data, if nothing else. It is important to understand that learning not to use a specific course of action a second time is always valuable, no matter the costs. Working to build this into your core trading mindset will lead you to greater success in a wider variety of situations in the long term.

Put consistency above all else: When it comes to developing a professional trading mindset, you are going to need to learn to prioritize consistency in all things. This can be another fact that is easy to understand in theory but much more difficult to put into practice. In order to get to this point, you will need to deal with financial setbacks and profits that were less than they first appeared. Ensuring these types of situations don't happen in the future requires a level of inquisitiveness that isn't innate for many traders. Making a habit of digging deeper into the reasons behind your successes as well as your failures is sure to lead to a greater level of success overall.

While certain types of investment market trading lend themselves to high risk/high reward strategies, trading options is not one of them. The best options traders tend to prioritize reliable gains of middling size and leave the riskier trades to the novices. While a larger than average return is nothing to sneeze at, a reliable trading record is going to generate a greater level of gain in the long term.

Understand your strengths and weaknesses: In order to find success in the long term, it is important that you understand where your trading strengths and weaknesses lie. Only by reaching this level of personal understanding will you ever be able to create a trading plan that builds on the one while minimizing the other. This is another reason it is so important to keep a trading journal as it will help to reveal tendencies that you tend to repeat that you might not otherwise be aware of.

Doing so will help you to become more aware of when you are letting emotions cloud your judgment as it will be clear when you made trades that you would not have made at the beginning of the day when your head was clear. With enough practice, you will then be able to head these emotions off at the pass and take a break instead of letting your successful trade percentage suffer.

Focus on keeping a clear mind, and you will find that not only is it easier to stick to your system but that you are able to determine the specific causes for success or failure found in each trade as well. Practice keeping this mindset during every trade, and you will see a greater percentage of successful trades sooner than you may expect.

Chapter 2: Tips for Success

Avoid call options that are out of the money: While most investment markets focus on the trend of buying low and selling high, this approach doesn't work when it comes to options trading. Putting your money on out of the money call options often devolves into little more than gambling, and there are more effective ways of gambling that have much higher odds of success. Additionally, making these types of trades can make it difficult for you to understand why the trade failed to return a profit which makes the whole thing an exercise in futility.

To understand why out of the money call options are a poor choice it is important to keep in mind that when you purchase an option, you are saying not only that you know how the underlying asset is going to move but also when that move is going to occur. If you make a mistake when judging either, you are going to be out the premium you paid for the option along with the cost of the commission as well. What's worse, your funds will then be tied up until the option expires meaning you may miss out on a preferable alternative in the interim. Remember, in order to see a return on this type of trade the underlying asset of an option that is out of the money needs not only to increase, it also needs to reach all the way to the strike price.

Know when to use varying strategies: Options trading offers up a wide variety of different strategies to ensure you don't end up trying to fit square pegs into round holes. For example, buying on spread will sometimes be an excellent way to capitalize on various market conditions, but only if you are aware of the specifics beforehand. Not only will focusing on a single strategy cost you money in the long run, but it will also skew your results by calculating false losses that were not indicative of the strength of the system in question.

Know the spread: A long spread is made up of a pair of options that are similar in every way except one has a higher strike price than the other. The option with the higher cost is being purchased while the other is being sold. These options can be either puts or calls. Long spreads comprised of calls are bullish, and those comprised of puts are bearish.

Despite the fact that when the time lapse hurts one-half of the spread, it helps the other, spreads ultimately hurt your profit potential in most cases. This is because one-half of the pair is practically always going to expire unless the underlying asset is extremely volatile. With that being said, if you are interested in reliability above all else then they are still a good choice.

Always have a clear point of entry and exit: To trade in the options market successfully, it is important to always have a clear idea of the ideal entry and exit points you are going to utilize. Not only will doing so help to mitigate the influence that emotion might have on each trade, but it will also ensure that you remain in the black over the long term. While it can be difficult to exit a trade when there is still the potential of money on the table, it is important to keep in mind that the potential for loss is also ever present. Setting a reasonable exit point and sticking with it is going to generate a larger profit over a prolonged period of time, guaranteed.

Avoid doubling up: If you are in the middle of a trade that appears to be going well and it suddenly turns around apparently at random, it is only natural to want to do anything you can to save it. Unfortunately, the best option virtually every single time is going to be to cut your losses and move on. In this situation, it is important to keep in mind that options are derivatives which mean the price is likely to change, and 'doubling down' is likely only going to lead to a greater overall loss.

While doubling down might feel like the right move at the moment, if you take the time to consider the amount of related time decay you are dealing with it can help to clear your head. If you still can determine what the right course of action is going to be all you need to do is to take an extra moment to clear your head and consider what you would have done in this situation if you weren't already committed. Nine times out of 10 the correct decision is going to be just to cut your losses and move on.

Stay away from illiquid options: Illiquidity measures the speed at which a specific option can be either bought or sold without causing the price to shift noticeably. Liquidity, on the other hand, can be thought of as the chance that the second trade of a given underlying asset will take place at the same price as the first. The stock market tends to be more liquid than the options market simply because there are fewer options related to each individual stock. As a result, you are automatically 10 percent more likely to end up on the losing side of a trade if you choose to move forward with an illiquid option.

Be willing to buy back short options: While, in theory, it might seem like buying back short options at the last moment is the best choice, this practice is sure to hurt you more than help you in the long run. It may be tempting to hold onto profitable options in order to squeeze the maximum return out of each investment, but you need to be aware that the potential for a reversal is always lurking in the shadows. Instead, a good rule of thumb is to buy back options that are currently at 80 percent of your ideal return or higher and let the extra take care of itself. While it may hurt to leave some potential profit on the table, it will improve your overall reliability, netting you a profit in the long run.

Keep earnings and dividend dates in mind: It is important to keep an eye on any underlying assets that you are currently working with as those who are currently holding calls have the potential to be assigned early dividends, with greater dividends having an increased chance of this occurrence. As owning an option doesn't mean owning

the underlying asset, if this happens to

you, then you won't be able to collect on your hard-earned money. The Early assignment is largely a random occurrence which means that if you don't keep your ear to the ground, it can be easy to get caught unaware and be unable to exercise the option before you miss the boat.

Along similar lines, you also want to be aware of when the earning season is going to take place for any of your underlying assets as it is likely going to increase the price of all of the contracts related to the underlying asset in question. Additionally, you will need to be caught up on current events as even the threat of influential news can be enough to cause a significant spike in volatility and premiums as well. In order to minimize the additional costs associated with trading during these periods, you are going to want to utilize a spread. Doing so will minimize the effect that inflation has on your bottom line.

Respond to an early assignment in the right way: When it comes time to sell the options you have purchased it is important to keep the possibility of early assignment in mind. To avoid unpleasantness, you are going to want to avoid lower-striking the long option in order to generate enough of the required underlying asset. Rather, you are going to want to place the long option onto the open market which will provide you with the chance to profit from the premium caused by the remaining time. You can then use your new funds to purchase the underlying asset that you are on the hook for, netting a profit in the process.

When you come up against an early assignment, it is important not to let your emotions get the better of you. Remember, the early assignment is more or less random so there is little you can do to prevent it from happening. Other traders aren't always going to make the best choices, and all you do is to roll with the punches. All you can do is to try and negate the chances of it affecting you as much as possible by being prepared for it depending on the mood of the market and its current level of volatility.

If you are going to utilize a spread, do it all at once: While purchasing a spread in a two-step process might seem like a good way to maximize profit, in reality, you are playing with fire. Specifically, purchasing a put or a call and then waiting to purchase the other half of the spread often leaves you open for the possibility of a reversal that will cost you more than what you would have made had things gone your way. Purchasing a spread as a single unit minimizes the number of variables that you have to contend with and increases your chance of success in the long term.

Take advantage of index options: Index options are a safe choice when the market is currently sporting a high degree of vulnerability. Index options are much less likely to experience sudden changes to a majority of news reports unless the results are extremely far reaching. The larger the index, the more likely it is that it will remain neutral.

On the other hand, if the market is in a holding pattern then you are going to want to consider short spreads on indices. In order to do so, you are going to want to choose an option pair with different strike prices in the standard fashion. This will largely remove time decay from the equation while also guaranteeing that you will make a profit as long as prices don't decrease.

Avoid making trades you cannot afford to lose: Regardless of how airtight your trading system appears to be, it is important to make it a habit of never investing more than you can afford to lose. No single trade is ever going to offer up enough of an incentive that taking the risk of knocking yourself out of the trading game entirely makes sense. Ensure that you know your limits beforehand for the absolute best results. In fact, a good rule of thumb is to never commit more than 2 percent of your total trading capital to any one trade. If you take this into account, then you would have to make 50 bad decisions in a row to lose all of your capital. If this occurs, you are likely focusing on the wrong investing and should consider your options carefully before continuing.

CHAPTER 3: MISTAKES TO AVOID

Not paying attention to the difference between implied volatility and historical volatility: When looking to trade successfully, implied volatility should be one of the primary ways to determine if a given option is priced correctly. Generally, the greater the amount of implied volatility, the more bearish the market will become and the more expensive most options sell for. However, historical volatility is just as

important when it comes to choosing profitable options.

Historical volatility should also be determined beforehand so you can decide if the difference warrants further study. If this turns out to be the case, then you are going to want to take the time to go back at least 12 months with the underlying asset in the question in order to get a good baseline for the current state of things. While this can be time-consuming, it will ultimately be worthwhile if you find out things are not as they initially seemed.

Don't ignore probability: It is important to keep in mind that the historical data that you have access to will not apply to the current trend that the market is experiencing at all times. This means that to be successful, you are going to want to consider the probability as well as the odds that the market is going to behave expectedly. The probability is the ratio of the likelihood of a given outcome. Taking the time to understand the probability of a given outcome can make it easy to purchase the right options at the right time in order to minimize losses related to an underlying asset.

If you plan on purchasing cheap options, it is important to keep in mind that they are going to be cheap for a reason. The price is always determined by the strike price of the underlying asset combined with the amount of time remaining before the option expires. Cheap options are typically cheap because it is unlikely that they will turn a profit before they expire.

Don't ignore delta: If the delta of the option you are looking at is close to 1 then it is time to create calls, and if it is close to -1 then it is time to create puts. If you are dealing with especially cheap options, however, then it is important to look for options with a higher delta as they are more likely to behave in an expected fashion. This, in turn, allows you to expect greater gains when the underlying asset begins to move.

Different strategies are going to require different levels of the delta to be successful. Never enter into a trade without knowing where the current delta stands and how it is likely to change in your chosen timeframe.

Avoid choosing the wrong parameters: If you are working with options that deal in front month contracts, then you are going to want to keep in mind the timeframe that relates to the expectations you have regarding the underlying asset in question. While some options are always going to look good on paper, it is important not to become enamored and risk buying into a timeframe that won't provide you with enough time to turn a profit. What's more, you are always going to want to maintain a realistic set of expectations when it comes to the way the underlying asset is going to move. If you choose poorly, then you can expect a wide range of fluctuation before the option in question expires.

Not using sentiment analysis: Sentiment analysis is easy to overlook which is unfortunate because it is a reliable way to determine the likelihood that a specific trend in an underlying asset is going to continue over a set timeframe. This means you are always going to want to observe instances of short interest as well as put activity and analyst ratings to get a fair idea of underlying stock price movement in the near term. When utilizing sentiment analysis, it can be easy to mistake actual results for the mood of the market. As such you are always going to want to wait for any initial gut reaction movement to clear up before making your move.

Not taking technical indicators into account: When working with cheap options, it is important to avoid making snap judgments as they are much harder to judge accurately compared those in the midrange. This is because cheap options that represent a likely sure thing are always picked up extremely quickly so what is left requires a deeper level of analysis in order to find the best deals.

Using technical indicators can then help to ensure that whatever you do, it is likely to end in your favor.

Not looking at extrinsic and intrinsic value: The extrinsic value of an option is the difference between the current price it is listed at, compared with what you are guaranteed to make off its intrinsic value or the amount its premiums will pay out, even if it expires or there is no additional movement from the underlying asset. Everyone always takes into account the intrinsic value, but the extrinsic is often left out in the cold despite still being a useful indicator. While the intrinsic value is likely to stay the same, the extrinsic value is going to decrease as the option gets closer to expiring.

Not giving commission costs proper thought: Especially if you are interested in high risk/high reward trades, not giving enough thought to your commission costs can significantly impact your overall earnings. If you chose the brokerage that you are using early on in your trading career, then there may very well be a better option out there for you. Remember, not all brokerages are created equal which means that you may very well be able to find a much better rate with only a little bit of extra research.

If you are fairly certain that you won't be able to get a better rate than what you are currently working with, then it is important that you don't waste your trading potential by working for returns that will be dramatically reduced by the fees you pay. A good rule of thumb is that you should always try to at least triple what you are paying in commission fees on every successful trade. This will ensure that you have some wiggle room for failed trades without it negatively affecting your trading capital.

Not giving enough care to your stop losses: While it is known that you should always set a stop loss on options which have a large potential for success, or those that are extremely volatile, many traders still forgo this step when the stakes are lower. While not placing a stop loss on a relatively cheap option won't lose you much by itself, getting into this habit has the potential to cost you a great deal of time. Unless you get in the habit of always protecting yourself on every trade, every time, you run the risk of burning through your trading capital much faster than you otherwise might.

Avoid trying to adapt existing strategies: While it can be easy to come to think of a successful strategy as a safety blanket, trying to use one strategy in all situations is only asking for trouble. Every time you decide to change the type of options that you target, or note that the market is changing, you will find more success by starting from scratch on an entirely new strategy than trying to shoehorn in something that no longer works as effectively as it should. While this will ultimately lead to you trading less overall, your results are sure to speak for themselves.

CHAPTER 4: ANALYZING YOUR TRADES

In order to determine if your trading system is as effective as possible, it is important to keep track of your trades and analyze the results about once a month. It is important that you don't overanalyze your results as otherwise a handful of good (or bad) trades can throw the entire average off and cause you to move forward in a less than optimal manner.

The metrics that you are going to find to be the most helpful are going to vary based on your trading style. If you prefer high risk/high reward trades, then you are going to be more interested in total net profit while if you prefer to avoid as much risk as possible, then your successful trade percentage is going to be more useful. Regardless, it is vital that you review and thoroughly understand a wide variety of different performance metrics related to your plan or your system before determining if it is time to try something new.

Performance reports: A performance report for a strategy or trading plan is an overall measurement of how it performs at the top level. A good performance report will reflect on the rules you are trading by and compares the results to an overall historical context. Also known as backtesting, this is a useful process to perform either before you begin using a new plan or once you have already started if you feel that the way it has performed so far is a fluke. Most trading platforms can generate performance reports automatically both via back testing and in real time.

The first part of any performance report is the performance summary which outlines the most important metrics of the plan or system in question. It is common for these reports to include performance graphs, trade lists, and periodical returns. They keep track of every trade that you make, the time and date it occurred, the type of trade it was along with any profits or losses that resulted from it in the form of a percentage of the cost of the trade. Remember, keeping an eye on weekly data might not be especially helpful, though quarterly or monthly data will allow you to see the forest for the trees more easily.

This information is especially helpful when you want to know not just what your trading result totals are but why specific trades played out in a specific way. When studied properly they can easily allow you to see how individual flukes can be turned into patterns. They are also useful when it comes to ensuring that you don't repeat disastrous mistakes a second time.

These details can be found in the performance graph displayed as either a bar graph that shows a monthly net profit or through what is known as an equity curve. This graph is an excellent way of gaining an overall idea of the quality of trades that are made over a given period of time without dealing with the noise inherent in the market as a whole.

Metrics to consider

Every performance report is going to include a wealth of data, much more than you are going to need in most cases. This can make getting started difficult if you don't know where to look. Consider the following metrics first and then dig deeper if you still haven't found what you are looking for.

Total net profit: The total net profit broadly determines the success or failure of a plan or system over a specific period. This number can be found by taking the total gross loss, adding it to the commission costs, and then subtracting from the total amount made from successful trades. While it is good to know if you are turning a profit, the total net profit can be deceptive as well because it won't show how often your plan or system was successful, just the overall results.

Profit factor: In order to find the profit factor of your plan or system you will want to start with the total gross profits and then divide by the total gross losses with any relevant fees added in. If the result is greater than one, then you can consider your current strategy a success. This number equates to how many units of profit you can expect for every one unit of risk you undertake. The higher the number, the greater the difference between your wins and your losses.

Profitable percentage: Also known as the probability of winning, your profitable percentage can be found by taking the number of trades that you have made successfully and dividing it by the total number of trades that you have made overall. Unlike with profit factor, there is no right answer to this amount as it is going to vary based on personal trading style. If you prefer higher risk trades, then a smaller number is acceptable. If you prefer more reliable trades, then you want the number to be as high as possible.

Trade average net profit: The trade average net profit can be thought of as how reliable your system is overall, expressed in the amount of money that typically changed hands with each trade. To find this amount all you need to do is to divide the total profit you have made by the total number of trades. If the resulting number is negative, then you know your plan needs work. When figuring out the trade average net profit, you will want to leave out any exceptionally good or bad trades as they

can easily skew the results.

CHAPTER 5: OPTION TRADING STRATEGIES TO CONSIDER

While throwing yourself whole hog into the options market means taking in a great deal of information in a short period of time, there are plenty of strategies to use that are likely to improve your returns and reduce your risk as greatly as possible.

Covered call: Also called the buy-write strategy, a covered call involves purchasing an underlying asset while also generating a call on the same asset. In order to ensure this strategy works properly, it is important to create a call based around how much of the underlying asset you own. This strategy is extremely effective if you own a separate position in the short term and feel that the underlying asset is either going to stay the same or decrease in value in the time frame for the option you created. When done properly, it allows you to generate a bonus premium at the very least. Covered calls are an effective strategy when used with index futures, LEAPS and on funds that are traded via an exchange and purchased on a margin.

Married puts: To utilize a married put, the first thing you need to do is purchase a specific amount of an underlying asset before purchasing a put that covers the same amount. This should be one of your go-to strategies if you feel bullish when it comes to the price of the asset in question and are looking for an easy way to minimize losses. The put that you purchased then acts as a price floor that can help prevent a dramatic drop in price. While putting money into an asset that you believe is going to decrease in price dramatically is never recommended, if you already own the underlying asset, then a married put will help minimize future uncertainty.

While a married put isn't going to be the right choice all of the time, when used sparingly under the right conditions it can be a reliable way to increase your overall success when it comes to options trading. To ensure that it always works out in your favor you are going to want to begin each transaction with a clear understanding of the risk in question. You can then factor in the added costs of a married put compared to the mitigation of that risk to determine if it is worth moving forward. As an added bonus, married puts help mitigate the potential risk related to early options to exercise as it ensures you always have available shares ready and waiting.

Bull call spread: To use this strategy, you will want to start by purchasing a call option at a strike price you believe to be beneficial. You will then want to sell a similar number of calls at a higher strike price. Both calls should have the same underlying asset and the same timeframe. This is a useful strategy to use if you are bullish on the strength of the underlying asset in question and your research indicates that the price is likely to increase in the time frame you have chosen.

This strategy is also known as a vertical credit spread because it has a pair of mismatched legs. Legs that are sold close to the money generate a credit spread that typically contains a net credit along with a positive time value. On the other hand, a debit spread is created with a short option that ends further from the money than when it started. Overall, this strategy is considered a net buy.

Bear put spread: The bear put spread is similar to the bull call spread but is used in opposite circumstances. Specifically, you begin by purchasing a pair of put options, one at a higher strike price and another at a lower strike price. You are going to want to purchase an equal number of each and ensure that they have the same underlying asset and timeframe. This strategy is useful when you feel bearish on the underlying asset in question as it helps you limit your losses if you are incorrect about the way the market is moving. This strategy should be used cautiously, however, as your overall profits are going to be limited to the difference between the two puts you purchased minus the cost of any transaction fees.

The ideal time to use a bear put spread is if you are interested in short selling an underlying asset and using a more common put option doesn't seem to be the right choice. You will find them useful if you are interested in speculating that prices are on a downward trend and don't want to invest a larger amount of capital waiting for the worst to happen. When using a bear put spread you are literally planning for the worst while hoping for the best.

Protective collar: To use the protective collar strategy you are going to want to start by purchasing a put option that is currently out of the money. You will then want to write a different call option based on the same underlying asset that is also out of the money. This is an ideal strategy to use when you have a long position on an underlying asset that has seen significant gains in the recent past. Using a protective collar allows you to both ensure the current level of profit while also holding onto the underlying asset in case it continues to increase in value.

Using a protective collar is as simple as placing the contract for the put option you purchased at a strike price that guarantees you hold on to a majority of the profit you have made. After that, you will be able to fund the collar strategy with the call option that you have written, making sure that it relates to a specific Digit. This strategy is a great way to maintain your profits while adding very little to your overall costs. What's more, it is very easy to ensure that you don't have to pay any related taxes as you can allow the option to roll over for as long as you deem necessary.

Straddles: The long straddle strategy is most useful after you have already purchased both a put and a call that share the same timeframe, underlying asset and strike price. It is useful if you believe that the price of the underlying asset is going to move significantly in one direction, you just don't know which direction it is going to be. Putting a long straddle into effect allows you to rest easy as you will see a gain as long as the price starts moving within the time frame you have chosen.

Alternatively, to institute a short straddle, you will want to sell a call and a put with the same timeframe, the same costs and related to the same underlying asset. This will ensure that you make a profit from the premium if you don't expect the underlying asset to move much in either direction in the specified timeframe. Be aware, however, that the odds of success will decrease proportionally to the amount that the underlying asset moves in the given timeframe.

Long strangle: In order to utilize a long strangle you will want to purchase both a put and a call that use the same underlying asset and share a maturation level. They are also going to need different strike prices. The strike price for the put should be somewhat lower than the price of the call, and both should be at a point out of the money. This is a useful strategy if you expect the underlying asset to move significantly but are unsure of the direction it will take. When used properly, you are virtually guaranteed a profit minus any related costs.

A strangle functions much like a straddle except that it tends to be cheaper as you are purchasing options that are already out of the money. This means you can routinely expect to pay as much as 50 percent less which makes it easier to play both sides of the fence. When given the option, a long strangle is preferable to a short straddle as it offers the chance at twice the premium while forcing you to take on the same amount of risk.

Butterfly spread: A butterfly spread requires the use of a bear spread strategy in addition to a bull strategy and contains three separate strike points. To start you want to purchase a call option at the lowest price you can manage. You will then want to sell two calls at a higher price and a third call at a price that is higher still. Your goal is to ensure a range of potential profits at prices you believe will be profitable. The most effective time to use a butterfly spread is when you have a neutral opinion on the current state of the market.

It is a good idea to utilize a butterfly spread when you expect the underlying asset that you favor to increase in price but are unsure of how much gain to expect. As such, you are going to want to make sure the overall market volatility is as low as possible. The higher the overall level of volatility, the more setting up a butterfly spread will cost you. The butterfly spread is not without a downside, however, as if you are wrong about the direction the underlying asset is going to move in then the losses can be significant.

Iron Condor: In order to use the iron condor strategy, you are going to want to start with a short position and a long position utilizing a pair of 'strangle' strategies to take full advantage of a market that is low in volatility. One 'strangle' is going to be long and the other short and set to an outer strike price. You can also move forward using two credit spreads. In this case, the call spread would be above the current market price, and the put would be below the current market price.

You are only going to want to attempt the iron condor when trading in index options because they offer a unique mix of increased volatility coupled with a lower increase in risk. Additionally, it is important to put an iron condor into play only when you are extremely confident you know where the market is going. This is because the potential for loss, should you choose poorly, is very great. Assuming all goes according to plan you then stand to make a significant profit assuming the market doesn't move strongly in one direction or the other.

Iron Butterfly: To start an iron butterfly you want to use either a long or a short straddle and concurrently either purchase or sell a strangle based on the straddle you chose. While similar to a basic butterfly, this strategy utilizes both calls and puts rather than just one or the other. When done properly it limits the potential for profit or loss to the range of the strike prices that you set. This strategy is best used with options that are out of the money as they allow you to minimize both risk and cost.

The pair of options that you use in the iron butterfly should be set at a mid-strike point to generate either a short or a long straddle depending on if you are buying or selling. The so-called wings of the butterfly are formed from the pair of options at the lower strike price and the higher strike price that are generated once the strangle is sold. This helps to offset the long or short position which creates the limits regarding your total profits or losses.

CHAPTER 6: ADVANCED STRATEGIES TO TRY

Double diagonal strategy: In order to properly use the double diagonal strategy, you will start with a diagonal put spread along with a diagonal call spread. You can turn a horizontal spread into a diagonal spread by simply shifting the long leg to a new strike point with a different timeframe. Any spread where the two legs don't use the same month is said to be diagonal.

When using a diagonal call spread, you will need to combine a short call spread and a long calendar spread to allow it to move based on the rate at which time decay affects the option in question. Once you sell off the second call at the initial strike point, you will have backed into a spread for the short call. This will allow you to create a net credit which means that after the second call has been sold anything else you make is pure profit. A diagonal put works in largely the same way with the specifics reversed.

To run a double diagonal, you will start by putting a diagonal put spread and a diagonal call spread into play. This will provide you with the opportunity to

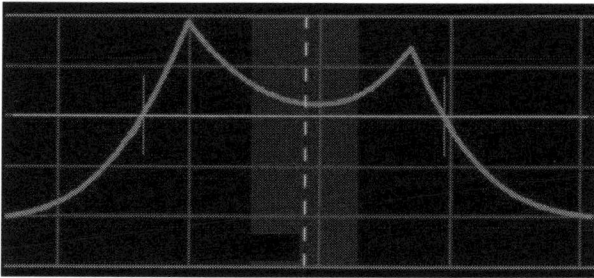

profit from the increased time decay that front-month options experience when compared with back-month options.

To do so, you start with buying a put that is currently out of the money at a strike price that will be good for two months. At the same time, you will want to sell an out of the money put at a strike price that is good for one month. Furthermore, you are going to want to sell a call that is out of the money at a strike price that is good for one month. Finally, you will purchase a call at a separate strike price that is good for two months.

If everything goes according to plan, then the underlying asset will remain at a price that is between the second put and the first call. If the price remains above that pair of strike prices, then you are going to want to sell the options that are one month out. At the same time, you are going to want to sell another call with the same strike price as the call that is two months out.

When graphing this strategy, it is important to keep in mind that the profit and loss lines are not going to be as straight as you might expect because the two month options are still growing concerns. Straight lines and hard angles can only exist if the options you are graphing are all going to expire in the same timeframe.

While this strategy might seem extremely complicated at first, it can be made to seem much more manageable if you instead consider it as a form of profiting from a neutral amount of movement in the market, simply spread out into multiple expiration cycles.

The most useful time to use this strategy is when an underlying asset is halfway between the second put and the first call, the closer to the true midpoint the better. If the underlying asset isn't at this point, then biases towards bullishness or bearishness can skew the results. If the underlying asset remains at the midpoint, then the options you sold will expire without generating a profit, allowing you to keep a greater percentage of the premium.

This occurs because the first put and the second call that you purchased will help to decrease your overall risk, even if the underlying asset moves more than you might like. The goal of this strategy is to leave you with a net credit, though this is not always how things shake out. It is not a sure thing because the front month trades inherently have less time value which means that a net debit is a possibility. If this occurs, then you can make up the difference by selling the remaining options after the front month pair expires.

When the front month pair is close to expiring, and the price of the underlying asset is somewhere between the price of the second put and the first call then you are going to way to buy close to the pair of puts and create an additional put for sale at the second strike price along with a third call at the third strike price. These new options should have the same expiration as the other two month options. This is what is known as rolling out, and it can easily double, or even triple, your profits.

Leveraged covered call strategy: Also known as the fig leaf strategy, the leveraged covered call strategy is a great way to mitigate some of the risks that come along with trading options based on Long Term Equity Anticipation Securities (LEAPS). A standard LEAPS call is not set to expire for at least a year which means a short-term call lasts about 45 days. This strategy is useful if you feel somewhat bullish about the market's chances over this timeframe.

To utilize this strategy, you are going to start by purchasing a LEAPS call with access to a profitable strike price for the related underlying asset. At the same time, you are going to sell a call at a favorable strike price to ensure you can make a profit if you end up being assigned early. The goal here is to provide a covered call for the LEAPS transaction. While the two options you have committed two are similar, the fact that they have different expiration dates allows you to maximize your profits when compared with a standard covered call. Next, you are going to sell a call that is out of the money in the short term at the same strike price as the call. Ideally, the underlying asset will then stick close to the second strike price and not the first.

This strategy is useful if you don't want to put up all of the required capital right at the start. This, in turn, means that the

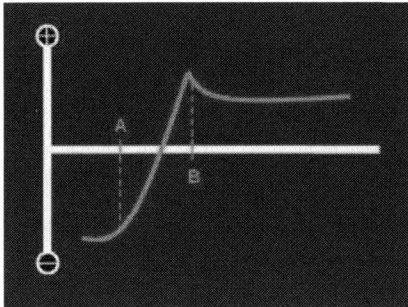

premium that is generated as you sell the call is going to represent a larger percentage of your initial investment, leverage will ensure your profits are proportionally higher as well.

When graphing this strategy, be aware that your loss and profit lines will not be straight as the LEAPS call is going to remain open while the other call expires. You should also keep in mind that determining what your likely profits are going to be is tricky, in this instance, because the available data won't be reliable until enough time has passed to see where the LEAPs call is likely to end up.

When using the fig leaf strategy, your goal should be to purchase a LEAPS call that is going to move in the same way as the underlying asset. As such, it is recommended that you only consider calls that have a delta of .8 or higher. This means you are going to want to look at options that are at least 20 percent of the money. If you are considering an underlying asset that experiences a high degree of volatility, then options that are at least 40 percent of the money are recommended.

While this strategy is more useful in many situations than a traditional covered call, it is not with additional risks. First, unlike most underlying assets, LEAPS eventually expire which is something you need to take into account if you are to keep your investment. Second, being assigned on the short call can be cumbersome as you likely won't own the underlying asset when it occurs. You won't want to exercise your option to buy on the LEAPS call because you lose out on a significant amount of time value. The best solution is simply to hope that the short call expires out of the money and that you can sell it multiple times before the LEAPS call ultimately expires. Alternatively, you can sell the LEAPS call on the open market to ensure that you profit from the time value that remains. If you go this route, you are going to want to ensure that you also purchase the underlying asset to cover any short positions that might materialize.

This is an effective strategy if you have a clear idea of how an underlying asset is going to move but cannot currently afford to purchase it directly. If the price of this assets jumps the first strike price and heads right toward the second, then you can make an early profit by closing out the whole option.

Skip strike butterfly call spread: The biggest difference between a skip strike butterfly call spread and a traditional butterfly spread is that is much more directionally focused. With the skip strike version, you are going to want the underlying stock price to increase, though not beyond the limit of your secondary strike price. The calls at the second and fourth strike points will be nearly 0 though you will still retain the premium generated by the call at the primary strike price.

This strategy works by placing a short call spread into a butterfly long call spread. Essentially what you are doing is unloading the short call spread as a means of paying for the butterfly. While this would technically mean that you need to buy and sell a call at the same strike price, the results of this transaction would balance out so it can be skipped.

The spread on the short call allows for this strategy to be arranged with little extra cost in exchange for the chance at a significant gain. This also adds risk to the proceedings making the skip strike butterfly call spread riskier than a traditional butterfly spread. In order to get the best results from this strategy, you are going to want to ensure that all of the strike prices that you use are equidistance from one another while also expiring in the same month. The price of the underlying asset in question should then remain at or below the first strike price for the best results.

To use the skip strike butterfly call spread the first thing you are going to want to do is to purchase a call at the primary strike point. You will then want to sell a pair of calls at the second strike price. Finally, you are going to want to ignore the third strike price and purchase a call at the fourth strike price.

This is a terrific strategy to use if you are primarily interested in minimizing risk. This is the case because the underlying asset would need to see significant movement before breaking past the strike point for you to see serious losses. The risk with this strategy can be further mitigated if you utilize it with options based on indices instead of stocks because many indices experience very low volatility as conflicting internal price movements often cancel one another out.

This strategy is especially effective if you are bullish about the state of the market as it currently stands and where it is likely to go in the time frame that you have established. As long as you hit the third strike price, you can expect to make a profit even if the options are going to expire at a point that would traditionally allow you to break even. In order to make the maximum amount of profit, you would want to exercise the moment the underlying asset reaches the second strike price. You will then make a profit based on the second strike price subtracted by the first and any related fees.

Skip strike butterfly put spread: Much like the skip strike butterfly call spread, the put version skews more towards a directional strategy than the butterfly spread version. The biggest difference between the two is that while the traditional version hopes for the underlying asset to increase, the skip strike version hopes for the underlying asset to decrease in value, though not beyond the third strike price you have established.

As such, this is a good strategy to use if you are a little bearish on the state of the market as you will not want the underlying asset to decrease too far. If things work out as they should, you would then make no profit off of the first and second put, but you will earn a premium on the fourth put. This strategy works by establishing a short put spread inside a butterfly put spread that has a longer timeframe. Much like with the call variant, you can avoid buying and selling at the second strike point as these actions will cancel one another out. Furthermore, the short spread will provide you with the opportunity to use this strategy as a way to generate either a small debit or a positive credit. Like its counterpart, the skip strike butterfly put is riskier than the standard butterfly variation, though the potential for return is greater as well.

To start using this strategy, you will first purchase a put at the primary strike price. The second strike point can then be skipped as the two purchases cancel one another out. Next, you will purchase two puts at the third strike price. Finally, you will purchase a put at the fourth strike price. All the strike prices need to be equidistance from one another and have the same expiration month. For the best results, you will want the underlying asset price to remain at or above the third strike price.

In order to make as much as possible from this strategy, you are going to want to execute the moment the underlying asset reaches the third strike price. The

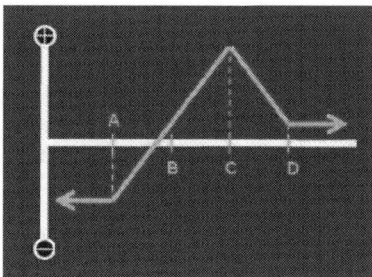

maximum amount of profit from this strategy is limited to the difference between the final two strike prices, minus any additional fees. In order to break even with this strategy, and still generate a credit, you will need the underlying asset to remain at or above the secondary strike price. On the other hand, if the trade was set up to generate a net debit then you will be able to break even at the fourth strike price as well as the second.

CONCLUSION

Thank for making it through to the end of *Options Trading: The Ultimate Guide to Options Trading*, let's hope it was informative and able to provide you with all of the tools you need to achieve your financial goals, whatever it is that they may be. Just because you've finished this book doesn't mean there is nothing left to learn on the topic, expanding your horizons is the only way to find the mastery you seek.

The next step is to stop reading already and to get ready to start trading options as effectively as possible. With the strategies and tips provided in the preceding chapters, you should have the tools you need to be successful regardless of the current state of the market. This isn't a sure thing, however, and only by taking the time to truly analyze not only the current state of the market but also the current and likely future state of the options you are interested in can you maximize your trade percentage as completely as possible. While it can be difficult to know the right move early on in your trading career, if you trust yourself throughout, then eventually that trust will be justified.

Just because you are now armed with everything you need to trade options successfully, doesn't mean that you can expect the profits to start rolling in right away. It is important to keep the right mindset, day in and day out if you hope to be a successful options trader in the long term. No matter how good you are, major windfalls are rare and chasing them is only going to cause your trading capital to dwindle. It is always going to be a better choice to take solid, reliable profits over riskier alternatives; remember options trading is a marathon, not a sprint, slow and steady wins the race.

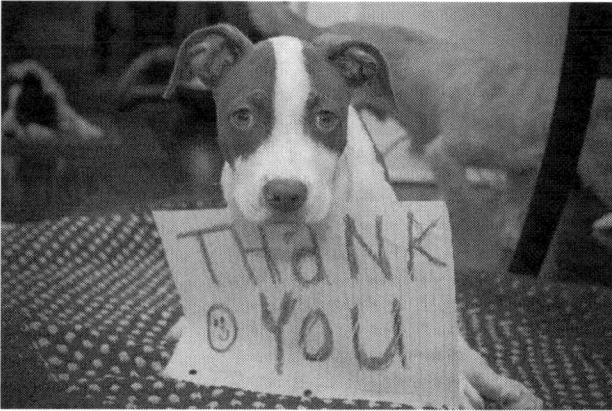

I would be so grateful if you please leave me a review ☐. I would love to get your feedback.

Sign up to my mailing list below to be the first to be notified of the release of my next book coming out shortly! ☐

Also when you sign-up please feel

free to send me an e-mail with

your opinion and suggestions. I

would love to hear from you!

Sign Up & Join
<u>Andrew Johnson's</u>
<u>Mailing List!</u>

*EXCLUSIVE UPDATES

*FREE BOOKS

*NEW REALEASE ANNOUCEMENTS BEFORE ANYONE ELSE GETS THEM

*DISCOUNTS

*GIVEAWAYS

FOR NOTIFACTIONS OF MY *NEW RELEASES* :

Never miss my next FREE PROMO, my next NEW RELEASE or a GIVEAWAY!

58594929R00177

Made in the USA
San Bernardino, CA
28 November 2017